DON'T LET GRASS GROW UNDER YOUR FEET TOO LONG...WEEDS WILL GROW

Real-Life Career Advice

By: Wendi M. Davis

Acknowledgements

I want to say thank you to all of my friends and family who have supported me through this process. Special thanks to my dear friends: Debbie and Sharon. Debbie, thank you for the inspiration to start writing this book. And to Sharon, who told me that I was an inspiration to her and encouraged me to continue shining my light. You, my friend, with these kind words, became my inspiration to finish this book!

Table of Contents

What Do You Want to Be When You Grow Up?

People start asking us what we want to be when we grow up from the time that we are itty bitty. Of course, when we are little, we would usually say a policeman, astronaut, fireman or teacher. As we get a little older, those responses may become doctors, lawyers or artists. In the teenage years, we are more apt to respond with "I am still young… how to do I know?" But then in the latter stages of high school, the pressure gets real. You start feeling the pressure to know what you want to do with the rest of your life…Are you going to college? What college are you going to? What major did you did you decide on….and list goes on and on. That is a lot of pressure! Let me tell you a little secret: It doesn't matter if you are 15, 25 or 45, you probably don't have it figured out yet and that's okay. If you have figured it out already, then great! But if not, rest assured, your path will be revealed to you as you start moving and growing in your journey.

In this book, we will talk about my journey – the experiences I've had, the things I would have never predicted, and all of the curve balls along the way. For instance, I am now in my

40's and if someone would have told me in my 20's, heck, even in my 30's that I would be an author and YouTube creator...I would have laughed in their face. Never in a million years, would I have imagined that those titles would follow my name. I had other ideas of what I wanted to do with my life, but fate had other plans for me! I will use my experiences and provide advice throughout this book to help you recognize signs along your own path that you may be on the cusp of a change and how to navigate the trials and tribulation along the way. We will also discuss how to hone the courage and embrace the unknown to help you pivot when you need to... even if you might be feeling a little fearful but still wanting to push yourself to do it anyway!

If you have read any of my previous work, you will know this isn't going to be the type of book where I talk at you the whole time. I am going to ask you to do some internal reflections and write down your thoughts along the way. You will need to make sure you have your Grow Book or simply a pad of paper, journal, or notebook and pen nearby as you are reading this book. I will explain why this is important later. Let's begin.

What am I Going to Do with My Life?

My mother told me that ever since I could talk, I've said I wanted to be an attorney. I have no idea where it even came from. It was like it popped in my head and that was it! That was what I was going to do with my life. So, growing up, every time I would get asked what I wanted to be, it would always be the same answer, "I want to be a lawyer." Time rolled on and as I progressed in middle school and high school, I was required to research and write papers on potential professions...and my dream of wanting to be a lawyer persisted. I eventually added that I wanted to become a judge, but you get the picture here. When I was a sophomore in high school, I made fast friends with my biology teacher, which today we would call her a mentor. She and I would always chat after school or sometimes during the school day. We talked about her life and how she decided to become a teacher and I told her what my dream was. As soon as she learned of my desire to become a lawyer, she shared with me that her mother worked at the local courthouse and offered to coordinate an interview with one of the local judges. Needless to say, I was ecstatic at the thought of this amazing opportunity!

A few weeks went by and I finally received a call from the courthouse stating that the municipal court judge wanted to meet with me for an interview. I couldn't believe it! I was now one step closer to fulfilling my lifelong goal (being 16 at the time, it was life-long to me). I was so excited about this opportunity that I could hardly contain myself. Time seemed to pass by so slowly from the time I received the call until the day of the interview. Then, finally the day arrived. I was so nervous about interviewing with the judge. I mean this was my first "real" interview. I had a job at a local fast-food establishment but this was the first interview I had toward my much-desired career path. Not to mention, this was an interview with a prestigious, highly-respected individual. I wasn't even sure I knew how to act in front of someone in such an esteemed position. During the interview, the judge asked me about my ambitions in life and asked about my home life, my grades in school...you know the usual line of questioning. The interview lasted about 1.5 hours and to my surprise (or shock) before the interview ended, he offered me a job!

Wow! I couldn't' believe it...I was offered THE job that was going to set me off on the path that I had always dreamed about. As the years droned on, I would watch the same attorneys and the same defendants come in and out of the courtroom each week. Keep in mind, I lived in a small town so it was the like these people who were on a never-ending hamster wheel. It slowly hit me...OMG, is this is what my life would be like? Do I want my life to really be like this? Seeing the same faces and saying (basically) the same thing over and over again... day in and out? When the answer came to me, it shocked me to the core...it was a resounding NO! Have you ever found yourself questioning who you wanted to be?

"You have brains in your head; You have feet in your shoes; You can steer yourself in any direction you choose."
– Dr. Seuss

If you have, you are not alone. Let me tell you, when I came to this surprising realization, I felt like I entered a cyclone... spinning around and feeling completely disoriented. It felt like I was witnessing an optical illusion...the ones that are black and checkered, swirling around and around with no end in sight, and making you sick to your stomach from the dizziness. My head is starting to hurt just thinking about it. Keep in mind that at this point, I had just started my freshman year in college. And now here I was, stuck in confusion with no clue about what to do next or how to feel about having my world turned upside down.

In the first chapter, I mentioned that you needed your Grow Book or a pad of paper and pen. I am going to start asking you questions and I want you to write down the answers as we move through the book. I will give you "Little Sprouts to Nourish" that are nuggets of advice I want to share with you on each topic and then I am going to ask you to do some self-reflection in each "Fertilizer for Thought" section throughout the book.

Little Sprouts to Nourish

- Childhood career dreams are important. But remember not to close yourself off to other possibilities by holding tightly to what you "think" you should do.

- Think about your strengths and things you like to do…This could be a hobby or anything that sounds enjoyable even if you haven't tried it before.

Fertilizer for Thought: Think about what you thought you wanted to be or do when you "grew" up. Write it/them down. What did you like about that career, specifically? Does it match up with your strengths and likes? Write this down.

What Major?

Back to the story....at this point I was still spinning out of control... feeling like I lost all sense of who I was or who I thought I was supposed to be. I know this may sound strange because I hadn't even started down this career path, really. To those of you who can relate, you get what I mean by this. But, for those of you who don't understand what I mean by this...keep in mind that I never even considered anything else for myself. For the majority of my youth, I had a picture in my mind of who I saw myself becoming and exactly what my career path would be. Here I was in my freshman year of college with my Political Science major declared, not knowing what to do next. The lesson here, my friends, is that it is wonderful to pursue your childhood career dreams but it is equally important to stay open and flexible as you grow and discover more about yourself and your likes and dislikes. I always advise people that no matter what age you are when you enter college 18, 28 or 48, to enter into their freshman year without declaring a major. This allows you to keep your options open and explore different classes to see what might pique your interest. There is no hurry and quite frankly, there is so much value in waiting a year before making a potentially long-lasting declaration by learning and exploring all of the potential opinions available to you.

To give this a little more context, I already had two years of government employment experience under my belt and where I came from if you had a county or state job, you stayed in it until you retired. That was winning big in the eyes of my little town and family. So, naturally, I was leaning toward Public Administration as my major. I mean, it was the logical choice, right? However, the more I thought about it, the little voice inside of me kept whispering "No." The internal struggle ensued. Have you ever had a battle going on within yourself? If you are anything like me, I am sure you have had several of these moments in your lifetime. If you haven't...trust me, you will. My head was telling me one thing and the little voice inside was telling me another. My head would say "you are supposed to be in public service so a Public Administration major makes the most sense if you want to progress in your career." Then, the little voice would say, "but what if public service isn't the career path that you really want?" I had a hard time even wrapping my head around that concept. The thought that I may not do the very thing that I felt drawn to do, left me feeling overwhelmed and ultimately, frozen in state of confusion and fear.

> **"Always go with the choice that scares you the most because that's the one that is going to help you grow."**
> **- Unknown**

Then, after painstakingly looking at every possible major and making a pro and cons list of potential career paths for each major, I decided on Business Administration with a minor in Human Resources. I felt this was the right decision because I could use that degree in public service or if I, for some ungodly reason, chose to venture out into the business world, it would be welcomed and accepted. The idea of leaving a public service track was highly unlikely (or so I thought at the time) because I had been so wedded to my childhood belief that this was the path I was "supposed" to take. These types of life decisions are difficult to make. Often, you feel torn and many times you doubt your own ability to make the right decision. Trust me – this is normal and you are not alone! This is all part of the process of uncovering who you want to be in the career world and identifying what you need to reach those goals. Albeit, a painful part of the process but necessary nonetheless.

Little Sprouts to Nourish

- Trust that you are making the right decision. If it isn't the right decision, there will be signs along the way that will allow you to pivot in another direction.

- For those of you who are entering college, consider not declaring a college major until your sophomore year.

Fertilizer for Thought: Have you had an internal struggle about your career choice? Write it down. Are you dealing with one now? If so, start with writing a pros and cons list.

Am I Getting Kicked Out of the Nest?

So now, I had declared my major and was still working at the local courthouse. I was feeling good about having chosen a direction (my major). My family was happy and I was happy. I was attending college 30 minutes from my hometown so I could attend classes in the mornings and continue working at the courthouse in the afternoons. Things were working well and I was in a groove! But let's just say that did last long…

After about a year and half of driving back and forth, my already beat-up little car was starting to wear out as I racked up more and more miles. It was time to hunt for a new car. At this point, you might be wondering why I am telling you this. I will explain the importance shortly…I promise. And then it happened… I found a car that I wanted to buy soooo badly. It was a black, Pontiac Firebird with T-tops. I have always liked fast and shiny cars and coupled with my tendency towards instant gratification, I was ready to do just about anything to make this dream car a reality. After talking with the salesman, I soon realized that it was too much for me to afford. I left there broken-hearted but hell-bound on figuring out a way to make that car mine. And so, I devised a plan. The college

I was attending had a night program for working adults. The plan was to switch into the night program and work full-time for the courthouse during the day. Dumb, I know but I was 19 years old at the time and I was determined to have what I wanted. We all know that our brains aren't fully formed until the age of 25. So, that's my excuse and I am sticking to it! Did you make any crazy decisions when you were that age? Ok… Back to the story…

At this point the judge had become like a second father to me so I knew I was going to have to sell this idea to him. So, I began to prepare my argument, talking points and all. After several conversations, he finally agreed to let me work full-time so I could go to school at night. Upon receiving the judge's permission, I ran right over to the car dealership and got that car! Yea, I was happy now. But I didn't realize what I was setting myself up for. It was extremely difficult managing a full-time job and going to school full-time. Shout out to all the working parents that go back to school. I have no idea how you do it with children because it was hard enough for me juggling work and school. But I soon found a rhythm and was making it work.

Little Sprouts to Nourish

- Go after what you want – if you want it bad enough, you will make it happen.

- Asking for a promotion is intimidating, but be prepared and expect a great outcome.

Fertilizer for Thought: Have you ever made a fast purchase or participated in instant gratification? Was the moment of happiness worth your invested time? If not, do not be too hard on yourself but take it as a lesson for the future.

As time passed, the judge would always try to convince me to be a politician. He would talk about my charisma and the way people were drawn to me and how easily I interacted with people, etc. But in my heart of hearts, I knew I didn't want to be in that spotlight and I definitely didn't want to wear a fake smile on my face most of the day. If I was in a bad mood, I wanted to be able to be in a bad mood. After several refusals on my part, he finally stopped pushing that idea on me. Whew, that was hard to do but I just couldn't see myself doing that. Have you ever been that position?

At this point, I have my fancy car, I am working fulltime, and I am entering my junior year of college and I'm feeling like I have found my way. Until the day the judge asked to speak with me in his chambers, as we had often done. We talked for a few minutes and suddenly he dropped the bomb on me. He told me that I couldn't work there forever. I was stunned and felt crushed hearing those words come out of his mouth. He said, "You are meant for bigger things; bigger things than this small town can give you. It's time to spread your wings." Just the thought of that made me cringe. Here I go again, into this deep, dark spiral. What do I do now?

"It's only after you've stepped outside your comfort zone that you begin to change, grow and transform."
- Roy T. Bennett

Sometimes, we don't recognize that we are in need of being pushed out of our comfort zone. But this is why it is so important to have people in your life who will recognize it and give you the swift kick in the backside when it is needed. Do you have someone like this in your life? If not, you need find one…FAST!

When I look back on my time at the courthouse, I realize that the judge taught me a lot in the nearly six years I worked there. These are the lessons I learned and still carry with me today:

- **You don't go to work to make to friends.** The judge stressed that not everyone is going to like me nor should I strive to make friends in the workplace. He often reminded me that I was there to do a job, do it well, and get paid. His position was that if I made a friend along the way, that was a bonus.

- **Everyone puts their pants on one leg at time.** This was a reminder to never be nervous about meeting anyone, no matter their stature or position. No one is better than you because we all put our pants on the same way.

- **If you are going to be a leader, LEAD.** The judge made it very clear that if I was chosen for a leadership position, I was to take it…even if I didn't feel like I was ready or prepared for it. You never pass up an opportunity – you need to take the bull by the horns and handle business.

Little Sprouts to Nourish

- Never be afraid to challenge yourself in ways that you didn't expect.

- You must live for yourself and make sure you are fulfilling your needs. Do not pressure yourself to be at a certain stage of life because you see other people there… you are on your own journey.

Fertilizer for Thought: Who pushed you out of your comfort zone? Why did you need to be pushed? What did you learn? In what ways did you grow from that experience?

Finally, I Have Found My Place, or Have I?

Once I finally got a grip on reality, I decided to go to a job fair. This is where I found my first state job and I thought I hit gold! I started as a lower-level administrative assistant for a prestigious, state agency. This state agency was one that had a lot of clout. It seemed very impressive to those in my family or anyone I talked to, really. I worked my way through the ranks over the course of about eight years. I was lucky enough to work in various departments that really provided me with a lot of experience. What I really enjoyed about this agency was that it gave me my first opportunity to train law enforcement on variety of topics.

I felt like I had finally found my people! You can talk straight from the hip with them and that is my go-to language… I was in heaven. I really learned to hone my training skills in these roles. I also learned to think on my feet and multi-task to the Ent-degree. This agency was extremely political. The head of the agency was subject to change every four years but sometimes it would occur even sooner if issues arose. I think in the eight years I was there, I had five big bosses' transition in and out. You know when a new top dog comes in, here comes new policies, practices and initiatives. Boy, I had to learn to switch gears quickly.

Little Sprouts to Nourish

- Never say NO to opportunities even if they aren't in your original job description because they will build your resume and open you up to new possibilities.

- Use every opportunity to hone your skills.

I thought this agency was the greatest thing since sliced bread. I fell into my comfort zone again. This time I didn't have someone pushing me to make a change. I CAN'T stress this enough...Make sure you always have this person in your life! Since, I didn't have this person in my life, I had to learn the hard way when it came to realizing I was in my comfort zone and needed to push myself out of it! I soon found myself going through a range of emotions every day at work. I would get so frustrated, then be raging mad. I eventually found myself having to fight every day to prove the worth of the program that my division provided. After two years, I was tired of fighting. Don't get me wrong, I am a fighter by nature, but sometimes the juice just isn't worth the squeeze and I was getting to a point that it was affecting my home life. I had two little boys at the time and I just didn't have much energy left at the end of the day to engage with them the way I wanted to. So, that was when I made the decision that it was time to leave this agency. Even though it was a hard decision for me to come to, I knew it was time to move on with my career.

"Growth is painful. Change is painful. But nothing is as painful as staying stuck somewhere you don't belong."
- N.R. Narayana Murthy

Little Sprouts to Nourish

- Figure out what your triggers are that are cueing you into the feeling that you're no longer happy or have become stale in a role.

- Realize your worth and be aware of when it is time to move on.

- Find someone who will continuously push you to be the best version of yourself and if you don't have that person… be your own motivation.

Fertilizer for Thought: Thinking back to a time where you were ready to make a change…what happened? Did you experience a flood of emotion? What pushed you to make a change? How can you recognize it sooner? Are you considering a change now?

Did That Just Happen?

Let's talk now about some the painful parts that happened along my journey. I am sure you may have or will come across some discomfort along your path too but we can't let these stop us from achieving what we are meant to be or do with our lives.

Let's just say that I have had the unfortunate luck of having horrible bosses who didn't know how to lead or manage people. If you have been in the workforce for any amount of time, I am sure that you can relate to this. So, let's take a walk down memory lane...

The first memory that sticks out to me is my first female manager. She would walk up to me while I was helping customers and slide her hand down my leg WHILE I was waiting on the customers. She would say she wanted to make sure I had panty hose on because it was office policy to wear them. Of course, I always had them on. But lady, if you have to touch my leg to even tell if I am wearing them.... Maybe you shouldn't worry yourself about it.

Another boss of mine had no idea how to manage people or show grace to anyone. When my stepmother died, I informed her and stated that I would need to take some time off. She agreed, However, after I left for the day, she contacted me to say that I needed to come back in and submit my timesheet on the day of my stepmother's funeral. Of course, I complied. While I was in the office, I told her that I would be taking my bereavement leave starting that day. Upon my return, she approached me with a disciplinary form stating that I never called off of work and that meant that I was a "no-call no-show" even though I went into her office and specifically discussed it with her. This was the first and only time in my career that I received any disciplinary action. She showed no grace toward me or toward any other staff member for that matter.

Little Sprouts to Nourish:

- Sometimes you will have bad bosses... it happens to everyone but realize you do not have to tolerate ill behavior.

- Always advocate for yourself. Do not let people push you around even if they are an authority figure. You are a person too and are entitled to be treated as such.

Fertilizer for Thought: Have you ever had a "bad boss"? What made this person a negative entity for you? How did you handle this person? Was their behavior justified? How can set boundaries for yourself in the work place?

Later in my career path, I had to deal with the complexities that come along with working for an elected official and what that meant when new leadership was elected into office. Before, this particular elected official took office, I had to testify in front of a legislative committee that he chaired. After my testimony, he came up to me before I left and made it crystal clear that he didn't like the program I ran. Fast forward to his inauguration and I went up to shake his hand. He remembered me from the testimony I gave at a legislative session before he was elected. As I was shaking his hand, he was rattling off statistics that he wanted from me ASAP. I shook his wife's hand too (this is an important detail). I quickly left the inaugural ceremony to go back to the office to gather the information he requested. Two days had passed and all of the staff were invited to his inaugural celebration. So, that night I stood back in the congratulatory, hand-shaking line...this time to give him the information he requested. As I shook his hand...I provided him with the information he requested. His wife was standing next to him and I went to shake her hand out of politeness (I mean I just shook her hand a couple of days ago) ...she said in an extremely aggressive manner, I have already met you and she put her hand down and refused to shake my hand. I was shocked by her tone and how she acted toward me. Come to find out, she thought I was a hoe-bag. I didn't realize that my new boss had a history of fraternizing with younger staff and having extramarital affairs with them.... Not that I was ever involved or even interested. Even though I can empathize with her, there was no excuse for how she acted toward and treated me.

On his first day of office, everyone was on pins and needles because we know that changes were imminent. At 9:00 am, my email dinged and as I read the name of the sender... I froze. It was from HIM! The email read: You know I don't think much of your program. Tell me why your program is better than the legislation I created. And, that is all it said. OMG! How in the world was I supposed to respond to that without offending him? Talk about being stuck between a rock and hard place.

I typed and retyped my response a hundred times. I finally worded it in a way that didn't say one was better than the other but that they were more of a compliment to each other. Nonetheless, he never replied so I must have appeased him, right? WRONG...or I should say maybe it did for the time being. The first time he came to visit the division I worked in to do the standard meet and greet, he asked for people to give ideas about whatever topic he was talking about. Every damn time someone would provide him with an idea, he would look at me, call me by name and ask if or why I haven't done something like that with my program. In reality, I had already done all the "things" that were brought up but that wasn't the point. It was annoying to have someone in that position constantly put me on blast like that EVERY TIME he came to the division. From the time of the first visit, other staff members would always say, OMG, wow, he knows your name.... That is awesome. All I could think was...Boy, if they only knew.

Little Sprouts to Nourish:

- If someone is treating your unfairly or pointing you out in front of colleagues this is not normal, and is, in fact, completely unprofessional.

- Being a person in power does not justify inappropriate actions.

- There will ALWAYS be some sort of workplace drama, try your best to stay out of it. However, if it seems relentless, you have choices to make: you can either leave the workplace or speak with H.R. so you can feel comfortable.

Fertilizer for Thought: Have you ever been a part of workplace drama? What was your part in it and how did you handle it? What did you learn from this situation that will help you in the future?

The last male boss that I will tell you about was a doozy. He was the king of narcissism. You know the type; the ones that are completely into themselves and think they are the greatest thing since sliced bread. This boss would make me stay late at work well into the night and even come in on weekends. I mean 11'oclock at night on a regular basis. One day, I was in his office with a couple of other colleagues and I was writing on his white board. I happened to drop the marker and I had a skirt on. As I looked down, he said you can go ahead and pick it up… we are all family here. Get the hell out of here! I just looked at him and squatted down appropriately to pick them up. The funny thing is, everyone was so used to his nonsense that no one even paid any attention to his extremely inappropriate comment. There were other similar things that I experienced while working for this man. But the one that takes the cake occurred during the late afternoon. I thought he had left for the day. So, I walked into his office to get something off of his desk and I reached over to get it and the next thing I feel is his penis up against my butt. He actually wasn't gone for the day…He had come back into the office and walked up directly behind me. I mean, seriously?!?! I couldn't believe that just happened…I was shocked. I didn't say a word and quickly walked backed out of the office.

Little Sprouts to Nourish:

- Harassment in the workplace is a real and dark thing, even if other people seem used to it… do not allow yourself to tolerate this behavior. You deserve to feel safe where you are employed

- You do not always need to comply with everything your boss demands. You are a person with a life too and need to make boundaries of how much overtime you're willing to accept

Fertilizer for Thought: Have you ever had a boss who did not appreciate your time? Someone who would constantly tack on more tasks for you to do? What are ways you

can implement boundaries professionally so that you have personal time? Have you ever been targeted in an inappropriate manner at work? How did you handle this? Did you document everything and if you are uncomfortable, immediately go to H.R.?

"Fear, uncertainty and discomfort are compasses toward growth." - Unknown

I wanted to tell you these stories to show you that, unfortunately, we all have or will have to experience similar stories and they may cause you to feel fear, anxiety, and discomfort just to name a few emotions. It is a sad reality of life. But one of the take-a-ways from these unfortunate things is what we can learn and grow from being exposed to these experiences. Here is list of some of things I took away from these experiences:

The way people treat you says more about them than you: Don't internalize the way people treat you. It is a reflection of how they treat themselves. You know who you are. Stand tall with that. Don't waste your energy worrying about them.

Set boundaries: physically and emotionally...even at work: Don't let someone treat you like a doormat. Set appropriate boundaries that work for you.

If you don't believe in yourself, no one will: No one can validate who you are or what you do. That comes from inside yourself. Own it and let your light shine.

Learn to let it go: Holding on to past fear or hurt will only drag you down. You will be the only one holding on to it. Because trust me, the other person isn't holding on to it, so why should you?!?

Don't get me wrong, there are good bosses out there that you can learn and grow from too.

I have been fortunate to have some really great bosses along my journey as well. You remember the judge from earlier? I was lucky enough to have him as a mentor in my foundational years and I believe that he truly shaped me into the person I have become today.

I had one female boss who was all about business. She treated everyone equally and demanded excellence without ever having to say a word. I always thought of her has a slightly intimidating Grace Kelly with dark hair. She always had style and grace. I was starting to have some personal issues with my marriage, but I never talked about it. But she, somehow, noticed the difference in me and she quietly pulled me into her office and provided me with support. This is something that I would have never expected from her. But it taught me you can be both a hard-ass and empathetic person at the same time. One didn't cancel out the other.

I had another emotionally intelligent and smart supervisor and she allowed me to grow Hond blossom under her leadership. She managed with a kind and gentle hand. Now, to be clear, I never mastered the gentle-part...I am more of a hurricane, but I did learn how to be more emotionally intelligent and how it was beneficial in the workplace.

Little Sprouts to Nourish:

- Realize the strengths of your superiors and learn from them.

- Recognize that they are people too with their own lives.

- Appreciate their efforts in trying to connect with you.

Fertilizer for Thought: Write down the names of people at your workplace that inspired you. Why did you choose these people and what about them stuck with you? Is there a way you can implement their strengths or knowledge into your own life?

One male boss became like a third father to me, (remember, the judge was second one). He took to me instantly. Under his leadership, leaders were able to grow and explore who they were as leaders and what they stood for. He and I also created a personal relationship. He would always stop by my office every day just to laugh and joke and check in about the ongoings of my life. He also would drop off a sugar-free Red Bull on my desk when he knew I was a rough day or when I needed a pick-me-up! Don't judge me here (I don't drink coffee, so that is my go-to caffeinated beverage). He would also always refer to me as Wendi-Woo-Woo because I was like a tornado when it came to handling business and he would always come to me when he had an idea to think through or needed something done. And, even though I no longer work for him, I still hang out with him and his wife from time to time.

I had another female boss that was REALLY hard core. When we found out that she was transferring to our agency, staff people who worked with her previously started telling me that I reminded them of her. Another one of my managers said that her and I would either get along great and blaze trails or we would hate each other and burn the place down because we had similar personalities. Listen, I know I am a beast when it comes to work but after I met her, I realized she was a beast on steroids. I liked her. We were A LOT alike I mean we could have been friends... that's how much I thought we got along. Let me be clear, we never became friends, obviously, but you get what I am saying here. Her and I could get things done quickly and she taught me how to hone more of my skills.

The last boss I want to mention is one that allowed me to flourish in so many ways. He let me create ideas and run with them. I was able to use my skills to help grow and improve the organization. He was hands off and just let me... do me... and I grew exponentially from it and I will always be grateful for that.

People will surprise you: I mean in both ways... good and bad. It's kind of like what Forrest Gump said, "Life is like a box chocolate...You never know what you are going to get!" It is true with people too. Look at people you meet at work, bosses and staff alike as a surprise...and you will never be let down because you won't know what to expect.

Learn to have grace: This means for yourself and others. People make mistakes... you make mistakes...No one is perfect and each situation may call for a different type of grace... recognize it when you see it and use it wisely.

Appreciate the journey: Don't get so caught up in the day-to-day problems or struggles that you overlook the beautiful journey that you are on!

I am sure that we all have had similar experiences with past supervisors but the question we need to ask ourselves is what have we done with them? How have you been able to use those experiences to continue your path of growth and development?

Little Sprouts to Nourish

- Embrace the unknown. Not knowing and confusion is a large part of the growing process. Lean into this experience.

- Walk through the fear and keep moving forward.

Fertilizer for Thought: What have you learned from past supervisors? Good and bad? How did you apply those lessons learned later in your career?

Is it Time to Make a Transition?

For various reasons, we might start feeling like it is time for a change. If you start feeling those winds of change, don't worry too much about it...it's normal...natural. It took me a long time to realize it but we shouldn't fear it. I know sometimes it is hard because we think we have found our groove but something, for some reason... changes us or our minds about our situation. If you start feeling this way, you first need to try to figure out why. What is causing you to feel this way? Are you bored? Need a new challenge? Only you can determine that. You may not know what changes you are needing but you just know that you need one. Once you start doing some self-reflection, you may find that something comes to you that you didn't expect or where you land with your feelings is surprising... you might not understand it at first but have a little faith, it will be revealed to you when the time is right.

Little Sprouts to Nourish:

- Become more self-aware to truly know yourself and your desires for life.

- Change is good, uncomfortable sometimes, but incredibly beneficial.

Fertilizer for Thought: What steps do you want to take to further your career? Evaluate your current position, what do you like and dislike about it? Where do you want to go from here?

There are a couple of things that we need to talk about here before we can move any further with the conversation. And, this is the negative self-talk or self-defeating narratives that we tell ourselves during this time. The first one is analysis paralysis. We all have probably heard of this term before but it is where we get stuck on analyzing every possible angle and convincing ourselves there is more research to do before making a decision. We have to make sure we don't get stuck in this phase for too long. I am not saying just jump into things without looking or without doing the necessary baseline inquiry. What I am saying is that you don't need to go down every single rabbit hole you find asking all of the "what if's".

Are you afraid of failure? Not even trying is a failure. If you try something new and it fails, so what. It is what you do with that failure that matters. What lesson did it teach you and how are you going to start applying what you learned moving forward?

Are you telling yourself I am not "FILL IN THE BLANK" here? We need to try to stop and take a step back to figure out who's voice you are really hearing. Is this an old narrative that perhaps you may have been told in your childhood? Once you figure that out, you need to learn to stop that narrative and create a new one.

But let me ask you something else.... what if it is amazing and you thrive? What then?

Now, let's take this a step further and say you get over analysis paralysis or any mix of the other things I mentioned and now you are ready to make a leap. Beware... you don't want just leap for leaps sake. But you are now feeling primed and ready to go on your next adventure.

Let's say a new opportunity is presented to you. I am asking you to press the pause button here. Not the stop button, just pause. I want to take a moment here to say that not every opportunity that comes along is something you should jump on. I mean you don't want to jump on the first thing cooking and live to regret it later, right? If you are a follower of my work, there is one message I will consistently tell you and that is to listen to the little voice inside you. And, I mean truly listen.

Little Sprouts to Nourish:

- Remember to not be too hard on yourself.

- At some point, we can all be overcritical of oneself but try to replace these thoughts with positive outlooks.

Fertilizer for Thought: Try to think of why you are having these negative thoughts. Is it something from the past? Write down positive, professional qualities about yourself and how they could be applied to a future position. Whenever you find yourself having negative self-talk convert it into positive self-talk. If you need help in doing so, check out my *5-S System to Love Yourself* book for tips.

Let me be clear here, I am not telling you that the first opportunity that comes your way isn't right for you. What I am telling you is to take a breath… Stop and really think on it. Listen to what your voice is telling you. You will know if it is the right choice or not. And, listen, if isn't right, that's okay. More opportunities will surely come your way. There may be some time that goes by before the next one comes along but be patient. Trust me, it will reveal itself when the time is right.

Now, when an opportunity comes along and you make the decision to move on it. Own your decision and let the adventure begin… you never know where it will lead you!

When I made the choice to leave what I thought was my "home," I NOT so gracefully stumbled into the world of juvenile corrections. This was one of those moves where if someone would have told me that I would be working in juvenile corrections at some point in my career, I would have never believed them. This was not part of the career path I ever saw myself in. Little did I know that this was going to open me up to so much more.

As I just mentioned, you never know where your next adventure will take you. I ended up working for the state department of juvenile corrections for eight years before another opportunity presented itself. I will tell you this opportunity scared me to death.

The opportunity that presented itself was taking my career to the big stage... a national one. The reason this opportunity scared me so much was because I was safe or at least I felt that way. I had over 23 years in the state retirement system, I was at the executive level of management and I was comfortable again. I was also a single mother that had stability in her job and good benefits. Not to mention, the world of public service was all that I had known my entire life.

The new opportunity that presented itself was to be an executive for a national, nonprofit organization that focuses on juvenile justice reform. Wow, I thought to myself...I could really make a difference by helping to shape national policy and practice in this area. But the non-profit arena was a world that I knew nothing about nor did it provide the stability I craved given that I was the sole provider for my family. But this opportunity presented one of those "I will have always wondered... what if" moments.

When you think about an opportunity and feel like this an opportunity that you will always wonder "what-if" .... Then, this is one of those times you might want to take a closer look. I believe that if an opportunity has that effect on me, that is a sign I need to do it. And, guess, what? I took my own advice and I took the job and I have never been happier!

"Never let the fear of striking out keep you from playing the game."- Babe Ruth

I want you know that I am not a big sports fan; But this quote is so fitting! We sometimes can talk ourselves out of moving forward because we are afraid. Afraid of change... the unknown... or fill in the blank here. But, if we don't move forward or even try, we may never experience what life has to offer us.

Little Sprouts to Nourish

- Trust that there are always other opportunities along the way.

- In most situations in life, you are never permanently locked in.

Fertilizer for Thought: What causes you analysis paralysis? What are you afraid of? What could happen if you succeed? Make a list.

Should I Create a Brand?

Let's pause for a minute. In today's world, we constantly hear people talking about wanting to brand themself or re-brand themselves. You really hear it if they are thinking about changing careers. And, I know this a big catch phrase that people like to use but, quite frankly, I just don't like to use this phrase or the insinuation that it gives off.

"The only person you are destined to become is the person you decide to be."- Ralph Waldo Emerson

I don't look at the idea of branding or rebranding yourself because I see phases of our lives...our changes.... as chapters in our own storybook. We all change and grow throughout our lives at different paces. Think about a book, every time a chapter ends or begins, it doesn't change colors or fonts...it's just time to move on to the next topic and I think that is how we should look at changes in our lives too!

This holds true for the idea of comparing oneself to others as well. I know as humans; we naturally are drawn to want what others want or have. But this is not something you want to do when you are venturing out on your own career path. Now, I am not saying you can't use people as inspiration. Absolutely, you should do that. I am a strong believer in the fact that you need to surround yourself with successful people that have or are what/who you aspire to be. This is one of the ways to push yourself to level up your game. However, if it moves into jealously, wondering why they have this or that and you don't ...that is a whole other ball game. If you are looking at someone and gauging your progress based on where someone else is at...That's a no-go. You should never want to put your story up against someone else's. This is not a healthy way to get moving on who or what you want to be. Worry about you and your path and you will get where you are supposed to be.... when YOU are supposed to get there.

I truly believe that we have everything we need to succeed. When the time is right, you will naturally show what is needed without using the dreaded label of "re-branding". I believe that you have all the talents inside you and they may just need more time to expose themselves. You will learn and develop over time how to bring these to the surface. Nonetheless, as you grow and develop into the person you were meant to be. Then, you will shine in your own light.... not in anyone else's forced, artificial one.

Little Sprouts to Nourish

- Be inspired by others. Do not make them your competition. You are both on your own journeys.

- Trust in the power of time and the benefits that come with it.

Fertilizer for Thought: Why do you feel compelled to compare yourself to that other person? What do you think they have that you don't? What qualities do you have that will make you successful in your own right?

Now, What?

Did you notice that after the first couple of chapters I stopped asking you about the "What" you wanted to do and focused more on the "Why?" The "What" is just a baseline for ourselves and rarely do we get the "What" right. Or, maybe you did and that's great. I believe the majority of us start working in what we think the "What" is at first but it eventually changes over time. If we can start off focusing more on the "Why" components of how we feel or what we are drawn to, we will be closer to being on the right path for ourselves. If we are only looking at the "What," we may be leading ourselves down a wayward path. But don't fret, that may happen from time to time...But, rest assured, you will find yourself back on the "Why" path sooner or later.

We also didn't talk about the "How" either. I did that intentionally; not because it isn't important, but because it isn't important RIGHT now.

"Every success story is a tale of constant adaptation, revision and change."- Richard Branson

Once you know your "Why," you will then start figuring out the "How." The "How" is the easy part once you have done all of the internal work of figuring out the "Why" .... Your "Why". You can use Google or look up YouTube videos on the subject until your little heart is content for the "How to" next steps. Once you are on YOUR right path, the "How's" will come easily to you. Don't get me wrong here, I am not saying it will be easy to accomplish...I am saying the "How" will be easy to understand. You will understand what you need to do to get there. So, don't be afraid to hop to it!

As we grow and change throughout our lives, our "What's" and "Why's" will change too. Depending on where we are in our life stages, dreams, whatever it may be. As you change, you will notice that your "What" and "Why" may change too. It may be subtle at first but then it will hit you like a ton of bricks. Think back to the person you were 5, 10, 15 or 20 years ago. Are you the same person? Do you have the same likes? The answer will probably be a resounding NO! And, you know what? That is a good thing!

Would you want to be stale and stagnant your entire life? Having no movement, at all? Keep in mind, we are made up of nearly 80% of water, right? What does water do...it moves. It ebbs and flows every second... of every day. So, we naturally move and change as we move through our own stages of life.

Little Sprouts to Nourish

- Stop focusing on the what's and start asking the whys.

- Evaluate yourself and what you want to do with your life.

- The answers to your what's and why's will continuously change throughout your life… this is normal as you are constantly striving to become the best version of yourself.

Fertilizer for Thought: What has set you back throughout your career? Fear? Doubt? What have you done or need to do to overcome them?

Who Knew?

I mentioned to you earlier that I always talk about our inner voice throughout all of my work. And this one will be no different. I had a bad habit of not listening to my inner voice and I had to learn the hard the way that it wasn't the right thing to do. Okay, maybe that is too strong of a statement… I would try to quiet it… or ignore it… or come up with a million and one excuses why what I thought what I was hearing must be wrong. Let me be clear here, these strategies NEVER worked long-term for me.

"Some journeys take us far from home. Some adventures lead us to our destiny."-C.S. Lewis

I won't put you through the pain of listening to all of my stories where I tried to do this but I will tell you one. For years, I would hear my inner voice telling me to write a book. Write a book… what?? No way!! I would scream this to myself. I can't even string two sentences together how could I even think about writing a book. Then, the little voice would come back around again telling me the same thing over and over again. I would think to myself; you remember your first English professor in college. You know the one who told you that you were a terrible writer and you should never pick up a pen to write again. This was one of those stop and figure out which narrative was playing. Let's just say at the time, I hadn't learned that lesson yet!

I just kept saying to myself that I cannot be hearing this right and I would push the voice aside again. As time went on, the voice became louder and louder. It just kept telling me to write a book, but I still tried to fight the internal battle. I tried pushing back and saying to myself that I didn't know what to write about...who would want to read it.... etc. Now it got to the point that my inner voice became down right relentless... to the point that I couldn't push it aside any longer.

I finally told myself, "Okay, I am going to write book". As I made that declaration to myself, the voice urged me to say it out loud to my husband and two boys who happened to be in the truck with me (yes, I was not in deep mediation mode here, we were literally driving down the road while I was having an internal discussion with myself).

So, I did just that and proclaimed it out loud to my family. My husband asked what I was going to write about? The boys just kind of murmured, okay. Then, I answered my husband with "I have NO idea" and he just looked at me and said okay.... I truly had no idea what I was going to write or how to do it, but I was hell bound to do it anyway!

Do you remember earlier when I said that the "how" will come easily to you once you get other things figured out?

Well, that is exactly what happened to me. When I sat down to write my first book, "What Cootchie Wash Do You Use?" the content came to me so easily that it felt like it was like was writing itself. Then, when I sat down to write this book... ideas for my third and fourth books started coming into my mind so quickly that I could hardly concentrate on what I was writing. I really had to fight hard to stay on task with this book because the titles, outlines and chapter headings of my next books were popping in my head simultaneously while I was writing this book. I mean that is an amazing "problem" to have, right? Who knew that by actually listening and acting on what my little voice had been telling me all along, would make this all happen so quickly? Well, now I know!!!!

Little Sprouts to Nourish

- Listen to your little voice.

- Trust yourself and your capabilities.

- Know that you can live a fulfilled and happy life... one that you carved the path for.

Fertilizer for Thought: What is your inner voice saying to you? Is there something stopping you from moving forward? If so, what is it? Write this down. What steps can you take to start moving in the direction in which you are being pushed?

What Happens When You Let Grass Grow Under Your Feet?

A friend of mine once told me that one of the lessons she learned from me was to not to let grass grow under her feet too long because weeds will grow. She went on to talk about how she was surprised by the way I would approach a new life or career change… Let me explain… when I was about to embark on a new change, I would meet up with her (or any other friend) or give her a call on the phone to tell her about whatever new adventure I was starting. I would just blurt out whatever it was and then quickly I would say, "Yea, that is what I am going to be doing now, isn't that great." I wouldn't give her time to even process what I just said. I would say this to her no matter if I have started the new adventure or not.

Do you want me to tell you the secret to why I could say that to my friend or not worry about how my career changes were being interpreted by my family and friends?

"A mind stretched by a new experience can never go back to its old dimensions."- Oliver Wendell Holmes

The secret is that I had already done all of the internal exploration that I outlined in this book before I would talk to anyone about my next chapter in life. So, I didn't need or want anyone's approval. I knew what I wanted to do and that was it. Don't misinterpret what I am saying... I am not acting like a heifer when I say that. I wanted my friends and family to support me but I already knew deep down what I was going to do next and there was no stopping me once I made the decision to do so. What is your approach?

If you have been writing down your fertilizer thoughts after each chapter of the book, you have been working on maintaining your patch of grass along the way by adding a little fertilizer each time your internal exploration took you to a deeper level of understanding what you truly want to do with your life.

You created lists and questioned various aspects of your life that will help to identify growth along your path. Over time, you may even go back to your lists and notice that you have changed even more and that's okay. You are constantly learning and growing into a newer, better version of yourself. Each step of the way you have become more self-aware and closer to understanding what you truly desire and now you have a better picture of what your "dream job" is.

Hopefully, you were also able to take some of my advice and fertilizer for thoughts to heart to help you along with your journey. The last two pieces of advice that I want to leave you with are: Don't be afraid to push yourself! This is the only way to figure out what you truly want out of life. And don't prune everything that pops up along the way. If your patch of grass starts having some weeds pop up... step back and give yourself time to marinate on those things and really think about them. And, yes, sometimes you will come to the decision to just pick the wayward weeds along the way of establishing a new turf and it okay... that is just part of the process. Only you can decide what is best for you!

"The secret of change is to focus all of your energy not on fighting the old, but on building the new." - Socrates

I want to be clear that I am not necessarily encouraging you to leave the company you currently work for or completely change careers. I am challenging you to listen to your inner voice to hear what it is saying. Maybe it is telling you there are other positions or opportunities within your own company that may be better suited for you...and, that's okay! It's great! I just want to make sure that you don't take my advice as saying you have to leave the nest completely. We all have our own journey; we just need to figure out the best course of action for ourselves.

Does this process ever stop? I don't know the answer to that. What I can say is... I hope not. All I can tell you is that I am happy and content. I love my life and career now and that my quiet beast (my inner voice) inside me is sleeping. So, I know I am in a good place now. But I won't know if there is anything else on my career horizon until the quiet beast awakens again.

What is your quiet beast saying to you? Are you listening?

Little Sprouts to Nourish:

- Refer back to your lists as you move throughout your career and reflect on your growth.

- Take time to recognize your accomplishments and truly feel pride within yourself for how far you've come.

- Continuing watering your grass and you will have a glorious field to look back upon.